W9-COE-593

Sports Cars

by Sallie Stephenson

Capstone Press
P.O. Box 669, Mankato, MN, U.S.A. 56002-0669

CIP

LIBRARY OF CONGRESS CATALOGING IN
PUBLICATION DATA

Stephenson, Sallie.
Sports cars / by Sallie Stephenson.
p. cm. – (Cruisin')
Summary: Describes many kinds of sports cars that have existed since 1900.

ISBN 1-56065-078-8:
1. Sports cars – Juvenile literature. [1. Sports cars.] I. Title. II. Series.
TL236.S735 1989
629.222 – dc20 89-25197
CIP
AC

PHOTO CREDITS

Chevrolet Motor Corporation: 14, 21, 23, 24, 25, 42, 43, 46
Miata Club: 31, 34, 35, 36, 37, 38
Geoffrey Hewitt: 4, 7, 10, 32, 47
Minnesota Valley Corvette Club: 12, 16, 18, 20, 27, 28, 45
Porsche Cars North America, Inc.: 30

CAPSTONE PRESS
Box 669, Mankato, MN 56001

Contents

26
SCCA
GOODYEAR

Introduction

It is hard to say exactly when sports cars came into existence. The first recorded use of the term was in August, 1900, when the Sports Motor Car Company of London introduced their twin-cylinder Sports Car. This car had a new scientific desigh. Also, it was able to average 35 mph over the dirt roads of that time.

By 1910, there were 46 different car makers manufacturing some kind of "sports" car. There were torpedo runabouts with bucket seats, and there were cars with sweeping fenders and roadsters.

The 1911 Mercer Raceabout was the fastest car around. It was not a common everyday car to take a person to work or to the grocery store. It was a sports car. Its top speed was 60 mph.

The fenders were very elegant in the curving way they swept upward. The driver had to get into the car on the left side because the shift and brake levers blocked the right hand entrance. The steering wheel was on the right side as they are in English cars. The Mercer Raceabout had a strange windshield that was round in shape. It was located in front of the driver, secured to the hood.

The Mercer had a four-cylinder engine which was very powerful. It had to be hand-cranked at the front of the car under the radiator. It took several twists of a large crank handle to start it. There were no electric starters. You had to set the gas and a magneto lever near the engine. The magneto set off an electrical spark that made the spark plugs fire. You had to inject a few drops of fuel into the cylinder petcocks before you took hold of the crank handle. Hopefully, the engine would turn over after one or more tries. Hand cranking was hazardous. It had to be done properly or a disaster would occur, such as a broken arm.

The Stutz Bearcat was another popular sports car. It had to be hand cranked to start the engine. The Stutz looked shorter and more clumsy than the Mercer. Stutz owners argued that their car was better looking.

The Stutz Bearcat had a very powerful engine. It won more races than the Mercer. Racing at this time had a direct effect on automobile design. The Mercer and the Stutz raced in such events as the Indianapolis 500 and the French Grand Prix.

After the first World War, the United States was making millions of cars. Most of them were just ordinary, everyday cars. There was nothing very special about them.

RADAR
WARNING
RECEIVER
ESCORT
RADAR
WARNING
RECEIVER
27
Miata
mazda
SCCA
PRO RACING
Castrol
BBS

It wasn't really until the Gay Twenties when movie stars and others invested in custom cars that some beautiful body styles appeared again.

Late in 1928 a super sports car was manufactured. The all new Duesenberg Straight-eight. It was announced as the "World's Finest Car." It had both speed and power and it could do 90 mph in second gear!

In the 1930's, for the first time, sports cars cost so little almost anyone could own one. Most of these cars came from Great Britain. These cars were the early relatives of today's MG Midgets, and Jaguars. The Fiat also appeared in Italy about this time. The Italians were outstanding car designers. Their cars have always been way ahead of the times. Fiats are still popular today.

Most of the sports cars in the middle and late 1930's were built in France, Germany and Italy. Interest in sports car races like LeMans and Mille Miglia led to revolutionary ideas in designing the chassis for these cars. Some of the new cars that were built were the Alfa Romeo, the Renault, the Jaguar SS and the Maseratti.

During the Great Depression and World War II most people didn't have money to buy cars. But the cars were still being made. Somehow the manufacturers managed to survive these hard times.

Following World War II, there was a small popular sports line made in Great Britain. It was known by the initials M.G. which stood for Morris Garage. People who collect sports cars have always been in love with them. The M type was a special sports-racing type that was quite small. It was called the midget. This midget could go around corners at speeds that would have been impossible in other sports cars. The Post-World War II "TC Midget" is the type said to have introduced the sports car to America.

A number of our great American sports cars evolved from the Midget in the '50s and '60s. For instance, the traditional open-top sports car was replaced by the enclosed coupe or GT. There was room for only two people in these cars. Some of them came with hard tops because there had been so many serious accidents with convertible tops. Later sports cars included a sun roof or a canvas cover with some rollover protection as well as protection from rain.

Cars of the 80's

From tiller-steered carriages to MG Midgets to Lamborghinis, the sports car changed with the

Castrol
61
JAGUAR
CAMEL GT
GTP
61
Castrol
GOODYEAR
TWR

times. In the 1980s there were more and more sports car enthusiasts than ever, from housewives to teachers to doctors.

Manufacturers provided many choices in sports cars. Improvements were made not only in styling and handling, but the 1980s gave car manufacturers a chance to apply computer capabilities. New materials were used in the design of engines, chassis and other parts.

In the beginning of the 1980s, many foreign companies made plans to export hundreds of thousands of sports cars to the United States. Cars were imported from Japan, Italy, Germany, Sweden, Great Britain and France. They were racy, well-designed, inexpensive sports cars.

Other foreign makes, competing in the '80s for the market were the small Fiat, Porsche 959, the Ferrari F40 and the Jaguar XJ-S Convertible.

In the United States, the American sports car industry was undergoing a revival with the introduction of the new Ford Mustang convertible, the Chrysler LeBarons, Dodge convertibles, Pontiac Sunbirds and Corvettes.

What triggered the resurgence was the flooding of the American market by the Japanese

AMR 962

manufacturers who came on the scene with great experience in technology. They exported many popular cars to other countries as well as the United States, like: Honda, Toyota, Nissan, Mitsubishi, Subaru, Daihatsu, Mazda and Isuzu. The Mazda Miata MX-5 in particular, was a low-priced, inexpensive sports car that was considered the best sports car buy in America. It came in three patriotic American colors: red, white and blue. Young people of the '80s loved it, just as young people of the 1950's wanted very much to own an MG Midget.

What Is A Sports Car?

A sports car is sleek. It goes around corners well. It hugs the road. When you drive it you think everyone is staring at you. You imagine they are green with envy. Maybe they are.

Sports cars can cost a lot. Not everyone can afford to own one.

A sports car may have a convertible top or a sunroof. This is so the driver can enjoy the sun.

There are usually two seats and two doors rather than four doors like a family sedan.

Sports cars come with automatic transmission, but true sports car lovers usually prefer a stick shift. The gear box usually has five speeds.

Sports cars were first imported to the U.S. from Great Britain just after World War II. They were made in large numbers.

Today's sports cars look like they are moving even when they are really standing still. The design is futuristic.

The Corvette

You know what a Corvette looks like. A Corvette is a sports car.

Corvettes have been around for a long time. The Chevrolet factory has been making them for nearly 40 years.

The first Corvette was manufactured back in 1953. What a sight it was! The design was way ahead of its time. It had a fiberglass body. The headlamps were protected by a chrome mesh screen. You could tell a V8 model from a straight six by the gold V on its side.

PEPSI
The Spice of Life
BLACK HILLS ARTCRAFT
BLACK HILLS SILVER
SOUVENIRS
SUNDAY
BLACK HILLS GOLD
GOODYEAR
MID AMERICA
BILSTEIN
ZORA 1

In those days, like today, when a car factory wanted to show off a very special car they would take it to a car show. The new Corvette was taken to the Waldorf Astoria Hotel in New York in January 1955.

Many collectors say the 1956 Corvette was the best Corvette. You could buy it with a hardtop as well as a soft top.

There was a fancy design on either side. This was called a side scallop. It looked like a V. They were painted in a different color than the body.

The 1956 Corvette was faster than the 1955 model. It could go from 0 to 60 mph in only 7.4 seconds.

In February 1956 the Corvette was entered in a special series of races. These speed trials were held on the sandy beach at Daytona Beach, Florida. The Corvette factory team wanted to see if they could beat the Thunderbirds. The speed trials went on for a whole week called Speed Week. At the end of the week the Thunderbirds had won some speed trials and the Corvettes won others.

Chevrolet had three cars. A woman race car driver, Betty Skelton, drove one car. The other two were driven by John Fitch and Zora Arkus Dontov.

POLYSTEEL
RADIAL
GOODYEAR

In the flying mile, Fitch ran fastest at 145.543 mph. Betty Skelton was next at 137.773 mph.

After that Corvettes raced in famous road races held in Europe. These races went through towns and on curvy roads in the countryside. The Corvette competed against the Jaguar, Mercedes, Ferrari and Porsche and it did well. This made many people want to buy a Corvette.

In 1963, the Corvette Sting Ray came out. This was the first Corvette with super headlights. You could press a button and they would disappear. At night you could make them come out again.

The engineers built a steel "**birdcage**." This was a special framework and it was very strong. It protected passengers if the car rolled over. The birdcage was built under the outer fiberglass.

There was a narrow divider in between the rear windows. This was called "**a backbone**." The 1964 Sting Ray didn't have the backbone. It was only available one year. This made the backbone very special. Those people who collect cars wanted to have this car. The 1963 Corvette is the most collectible model.

Every spring there is a Corvette Expo in Knoxville, KY. This is the largest Corvette auction in the

Stroh's
BLACK HILLS
CORVETTE CLASSIC

world. It is the first major Corvette sales event of the year. It sets what the prices will be like for the rest of the year.

Bidders come from all over the world to buy a new or used Corvette. You can also buy Corvette parts for your car.

After the auction there is a Diamond Awards show. Show quality Corvettes compete for diamond rings.

In 1968, the Sting Ray era was over. It had lasted from 1963-1967. The Corvette came out with a new body. It had the muzzle of a shark and this style lasted through 1973.

The corvette looked great, but the fiberglass body panels did not fit well. The coupe with the T-shaped top let rain in. It was rough on the road and the noise was bad. The engine got too hot and there were other minor problems. This upset many owners and the engineers had to fix the problems.

In 1981, the Chevrolet factory moved from St. Louis, Missouri to Bowling Green, Kentucky. A Special Edition Corvette came out that same year. The color was Bowling Green.

CHEVROLET
CORVETTE
CHALLENGE
EXXON
MID AMERICA
GLOY SPORTS
SCCA
PRO RACING
BOSCH
BILSTEIN

GOODYEAR
HENDRICK
MOTORSPORTS
CORVETTE
22
GM
Goodwrench
BBS

There was no 1983 Corvette because Chevrolet wanted to get the new 1984 car out as soon as possible. It was competing against Porsche and Ferrari. A Corvette in those days cost about half their price.

Today's Corvette body style came out in 1984. It was faster and lightweight aluminum was added to the fiberglass. There was more space inside. The 1984 cars could go 140 mph.

Soon, it will be 40 years that Corvettes have been around. They have come a long way since 1953.

In the current Corvette Challenge racing series, Corvette competes against international sports cars. The engineers learn from these races. They see what happens to the cars they design and they learn how to build better cars.

Over the years Corvette has been in the winner's circle at many kinds of sports car races.

If you have an old Corvette you can belong to a club. **The National Corvette Restorers Society (NCRS).**

Many Corvette owners belong to the **National Council of Corvette Clubs** (NCCC).

POLYSTEEL RADIAL
GOODYEAR

The club also holds rallies. They are run on public roads. The contestants have to follow instructions and they are told to travel at certain speeds. There are clues they have to follow and they must complete the course in the time it took the **rallymaster**. This is the person who planned the rally.

Porsche 911

The basic appearance of a Porsche 911 has not changed since it was born in 1963. The rear engine is located behind the rear axle and it even looks like the original design. It had a 130 horse-power 2-litre engine and it could barely go more than 124 mph. The basic design came from its old relative the Volkswagon Beetle. The engine weight was in the rear. It was easy to spin out around bumpy corners. The steering was lively but you had to grip the wheel strongly. It had a jerky suspension and the gears were stiff to move.

Thirteen years later, in 1976, the 911 had grown to a 3-liter, 260 hp. turbo engine. Its power doubled.

In 1988, the Porsche Turbo had grown even more. Now it was a 3.3-liter engine. It had 288 hp. and the maximum speed was 161 mph.

Carrera

The 911 was one of the fastest **production cars** in the world. Production means that the car was not souped up. It was the way it came from the factory.

In 1989 the Porsche 911 was turned into a totally new 911. This car was called the Carrera 4.

It had 4-wheel drive so it had better traction in all weather. This car didn't spin out as easy. The engine was 3.6 liters and it could go 163 mph without a turbocharger.

Today in 1991, there is a new 911. The Turbo III has the latest 911 shape. It has the rounded nose and tail of the Carrera 4. It also has a turbocharger.

If Porsche is your favorite car, you can buy a 911 Carrera Cabriolet. The 911 Carrera Cabriolet sells for $15,000.

The Miata

The MX-5 Miata is made by Mazda. It comes in red, white and blue or it also comes in silver. You can put the top down. You can take it on a picnic. You can go on the open, winding roads. It is not an expensive sports car.

MIATA
NORTH CAROLINA

mazda
Miata
SIMPSON
95
Simpson Bros. Racing
East Coast Auto
Valvoline
YOKOHAMA TIRES
SCCA SOLO II
mazda
SCCA
SOLO EVENTS

In 1990 Mazda brought about 20,000 Miatas to America from Japan. That number is expected to double in 1991.

The Miata is a friendly, outgoing car. When the engineers built the Miata they picked a special engine. The engine is called B6-DOHC.

The Miata is a front-engine, rear-drive, convertible, sports car.

It is a soft top that latches to the top of the windshield. You can buy a hardtop as well. It weighs about forty-five pounds. You can store the hardtop in your garage.

You can join the Miata Sports Club. They hold group get togethers and have autocross and rally events. Members wear special T-shirts. They have a Miata magazine and even have a Miata calendar.

The Countach!

The Countach is one of THE sports cars.

It has a V12 engine. There are 375 horsepower in the cockpit. The doors swing upwards and forwards.

The middle of the cockpit is filled by the gearbox. It is enclosed in a large arm that curves up to form an armrest.

The Countach was made at the Ferruccio Lamborghini factory in Italy.

In the 80s, Lamborghini learned of the new Ferrari Testarossa. He wanted to make a faster car. The result was the 500 Quattrovalvo that came out in March of 1985. This Countach became known as the Super Countach.

The Countach was made to go fast like a race car. When the Countach was road tested it proved it could go 190 mph. It is said that the Super Countach could outperform the driver.

In April, 1987, the Chrysler Corporation acquired Lamborghini. They still use Super Contach in their research. But in 1990 a new Lamborghini came out. It is called the Diablo.

The Future

The 1980s produced many sports cars. The only time that more were produced was in the 1960s. In the 1990s there will be many more produced. Computers will design every aspect of cars today. Car designers are already at work on tomorrow's cars.

Sports cars will still be beautiful. They will still be fast. But they will probably not look much like today's sports cars. And they will not be powered the same. In the future, sports cars may be solar- or electric-powered. They may be powered by nuclear power, wind power or steam generators. Engineers have even thought of using recycled garbage and waste products to power all cars.

They will have lots of new features. Maybe the sports cars of the future will have a computer to do the driving for you!

Why don't you take out a paper and pencil. Draw a picture of what you think sports cars will look like. Will your Dream Car be long and low to the ground? How will it be powered? How fast will it go?

Look at this picture 20 years from now and see if you still think your Sports Car is the best sports car around.

ESCORT
Mobil

EXXON
SCCA
PRO RACING
32
GOODYEAR
PBR

For More Information

For a technical data poster of the Evolution of 1953-1990 Corvettes, you may call Ecklers' Corvette Parts at 1-800-327-4868. The cost is $5.95 plus shipping charge or write to P.O. Box 5637, Titusville, FL 32780.

You can subscribe to Vette Vues Magazine, The Corvette Enthusiast's Magazine by writing P.O. Box 76270 Sandy Springs, GA 30328. One year is $20.

If you are a Porsche owner you can belong to the Porsche Club of America. Annual dues are $36. You receive the monthly Porsche Panorama Magazine. The Porsche Club has more than a hundred and twenty chapters. They have driver education classes. They hold rallies, autocrosses and tours. They even hold a convention once a year.

You can belong to a club that races sports cars. The **Sports Car Club of America** (SCCA).

The SCCA holds special events. Some are held in parking lots that are marked off to keep spectators away from where cars race.

MINNESOTA VALLEY
CORVETTE CLUB

In solo events one driver at a time competes. He or she races against the clock and tries to get through the course fast. Usually, the driver races around bright orange pylons. The fastest driver wins. The SCCA holds many of these events. They are called gymkhanas, autocrosses, slaloms, traloms and field trials.

GOODYEAR
FIBERITE
ICI
ERITE
ICI
KENWOOD
TOYOTA
98
Wild THING

Glossary

Birdcage: Special framework strong enough to protect passengers if a car rolls over.

Backbone: A narrow divider between the rear windows. Backbones are only in 1963 Corvettes.

NCCC: National Council of Corvettes Club. Any corvette owner can belong to this club.

NCRS: National Corvette Restorers Society. A club that owners of old model Corvettes can belong to.

Production Cars: A car that is not souped up or customized. It is the same as it was when it came from the factory.

Rallymaster: The person in charge of planning the race course at a rally.

SCCA: Sports Car Club of America. A club that holds special sports car events.